TILT /
HOVER
/ VEER

Mary Newell

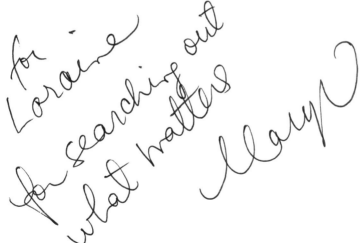

CODHILL

New Paltz, New York

CODHILL

Codhill books are published by David Appelbaum for Codhill Press

First Edition
Printed in the United States of America
Copyright © 2019 by Mary Newell

ISBN 978-1-949933-01-7

Cover and text design by Alicia Fox

ACKNOWLEDGMENTS

The author would like to express deep gratitude to the editors of the publications in which the following poems have appeared:

"In the pith of break down," "In the pith of attenuation," and "In the pith of a misplaced suspicion" appear in *BlazeVox* issue 18.

"In the pith of hover," "in the pith of swerve," and "in the pith of diapause" appear on *Dispatches from the Poetry Wars.*

"In the pith of luscious" and "In the pith of afterdays" accepted by *WoodCoin Magazine.*

"In the pith of fledge" (May) and "The wake of an ending" (with the title "In the pith of wake") (July) appear on *First Literary Review—East.*

"In the pith of a sad meander" appeared in *Clockwise Cat.*

CONTENTS

TILT

earth wobble
shuffles the seasons

In the pith of diapause

tone held through the gap
between crawl-chew
and flutter-sip

weather churn

on the brink: wings rolled
ready, colors soft
through chrysalis wrap

slow unfurl

finding the updraft

Note: Diapause is a temporary developmental arrest that allows insects to circumvent adverse environmental conditions, usually weather.

In the pith of tilt

    stacked wood

        moss green under snow

            tree's heat

              melts rings around the base

                covert stirrings

                push for sun and air

               listen forward:

               hemisphere tilts sunward

            daylight stretches

         spring blazes out

     moss plush

   between toes

Intersection Witness

Say the wakes of a sailboat
and a plump of mallards intersect:
many v's flange out behind their gliding.
Plankton, pushed to the v-arms,
roll over with turbulence, spuming.
while in between, the water is slick.

The wakes run interference on the tide,
deforming waves that lap the shore.

Say someone standing on shore
tries to unravel that rippling skein,
tracing backwards from the waves,
while her rapt companion
sways to the undulations
as the laps refresh her feet.

In the pith of intersecting wakes
say life is complex, perplexing—

has beauty, has pattern,
has meaning…
somewhere within that tangle
or in its witnessing.

In the pith of evanescence

from equinox to solstice and again

in circuits grand and paltry
>   *ticking away*

trudge through quagmires
>   *any-toned chronometer runs true*

rejoice in peak conjunctions
>   *sundial's slow rotation*

rush or drag through dry spells
>   *stopwatch marks unstoppable time*

glide through paradisal asymptotes
>   *ah, the interlude, the present*

this fleeting
>   *hourglass concedes to gravity*

heart's pendulum wearies

sight to: home

>   horizon

>   the spaciousness beyond

5

In the pith of afterglow

the slow slide into darkness
prolongs the breath

between twilight and sun blush
silhouettes loom, flatten

dusk the letting go of shapes
deep night, enormity

velvet cloaks the forest
opaque, almost strokable

sometimes the stars…
and just before dawn

a quivering

The wake of an ending
    laps hearts-edge
    nudges the tide toward shores
    where pebbles glisten salty

In the pith of swerve

The new sidles in
between the hinges

knows your name

recites arcane instructions

dissolves into mist when you ask for clarity.

The swerve astounds with its flare

    but means to unseat you

hiding
    within your site

peeping
    through barricades

seeking only

to bloom.

HOVER

an oscillative poise
a steady eye

In the pith of hover

When we stand still,   /stay still
      our heads' weight tilts us forward.   /inclines
      Momentum prompts movement
      to resist falling.

Wing flaps let some birds hover:

      a strenuous mid-air suspension

kestrel matches wind speed head-on
      poised in transparency to foresee

osprey hangs still to focus on foraging   /pauses, suspended

hummingbird parades his ball-and-socket shoulder joint
      his wing lift on up-beats as well as down
      skates figure eights before
      the trumpet flower's throat
      sips deep   flashes luminescence   wheels away

We are left staring at vacancy   /a blank
      sensing wake turbulence,
      vortex from activated wings.

Sometimes we wait alert,   /wait expectant, attentive
      thirsty for an intimation,   /hungry for a clue
      an evanescent summons—

      wait

just in case.

In the pith of attenuation

excruciate at the crossroads

      chiasmic tangle   climacteric muddle

      Janus-pull   cross-wires   warp-wrap

heed elusive

      scale-nuance   interval trill   attune

      consonance-throb

murmuration

In the pith of glide

Mallards' smooth glide
slices   river shimmer.

Below the surface
rapid propulsion ensemble

In the pith of luscious

      tongue-roll

      silk swirl

           frothy shoals

           tadpole twists

      pearl retrieval

luxuriate in

peaches

In the pith of watershed

                              We enter this world floundering
                              stripped of the amniotic sac
                              cold air, the separation

                    *

          vast boundless flux

                                        bearings

       To float with the current is unreliable.

Once a sea parted for safety
for passage to a honeyed land.
A whole community found refuge.

But now each seeks a way
through new wilds and currents   whirlpools   sinkholes

                    *

          The waters divide.

One branch seeps into sand
       gradual trickle away
One flows to the far-off sea
       each drop a reflecting whole

                    *

                    to see from above,
                    a sense of order

*

to resist momentum,

              to leap across
              glide upstream

                              for a moment   fleetingly...

and then?

14

In the pith of a sad meander

untranslatable starlight

punctures remonstrance

tenders unguent of

silence

proliferates

Peregrination: into the pith

To seek the tongues of inwardness
      the slightest stir invites
      a deeper listening

Detour for hints, for evidence
      too tenuous for clinging:
      ingress to the enigmatic

To heed a wordless invocation
      attune to overtones of
      reciprocity, expanse

To retrace footprints
      just here—and here—
      the route back, subtly altered

Many pathways wind toward home

VEER

aim for the polestar
wake up awry

In the pith of origin

A pulsing gelatinous mesh
buffered in warm wobble-drifts

Suspended, then thrust out – lifeline
severed, tied up and tucked away

Breath reticent in estranging air,
barraged by smog, electronic hiss

Wedged in the muck of aggregation,
dense attractors quell sidereal yearnings:

quicksand promises, polestar simulacrums
strangulating options, the pull of the void—

A love-pulse persists around the tatters,
unperturbed, offering succor in dire need.

Beneficence ripples through the silence,
imperceptibly, like stardust wafting by.

In the pith of remonstrance

*

Thoughts churn,
regurgitate.

*

Interior moon tangled
in the circumstantial.
The spotted sun flares.

*

Jaw holds tight
Exit blocked again

*

Meditation tempers impulses
but they sneak out,
run with blinders on.

*

A dog bites his own tail,
turns in narrowing circles

*

No whole from
bit parts.

In the pith of veer

The perfect circle:
completion, unity…
Where outside geometry?
Earth's axis marks an oval,
tilts and wobbles.

Blindfolded, most circle back
to where they started:
the tilt from a slightly longer leg
creates a swerve, nudges toward a circle
in roughly half an hour.

On the verge of getting somewhere
that slight deflection   a moment's inattention
a stray remark   a bright distraction

a veer

to end up
here,
back where we know the ropes
that hold us.

Can circle   morph into spiral
in time, in time?

....

"Among the majority of people, the full blindfolded deviation circle is formed in about half an hour." Harold Gatty, *Finding Your Way on Land or Sea.*

**In the pith of
break down**

Rose draws in petals
at dusk, forgets
to relinquish clutch at sunrise.

The world a rack
stretched pervious
or unbearable

shatter

      breakout

rally

A plea for kintsugi:
cracks filled precious
meander fusion sheen

luster reclaim
gold or platinum
neat or overflow

gratitude for
the flow that
seals the ruptures.

Note: Kintsugi (金継ぎ, きんつぎ, "golden joinery") is the Japanese art of repairing broken pottery with lacquer mixed with powdered gold, silver, or platinum.

In the pith of ricochet

rejoinder flusters the air

recoil   recalibrate

dither

improvise   rally round

     let the cards

          fall

In the pith of afterdays

snow-pocks

      wind-scatter

            lint-retrieval

            doleful read-out

      candor quaint

customs remembered in sketch,

      deflections

            without conviction of purpose

revived with plans for the yet-to-be -

the present still hard to imagine

In the pith of
hallow

Amid the ravaging,
the hollow of loss,

uncrate
what you held sacred.

Cherish
the gleanings.

COUNTER-VEER

amid fluctuations
an axis affirmed

In the pith of solitude

between silence and sequestered

declinations of serene

venture lightly past logistics

searchlight misses owls and morels

in the dark, measured footfalls

ears tune wider

soundscape wilding

poised

In the pith of saturation

raindrops evaporate from windows
the view refreshed

sunspark   ignites the leaves,
    pierces petals -
        translucent rubies set ablaze

a pause between thoughts,
    ethereal yearning

ribs rise,
absorb the air the leaves release, the rays—
    breath deepens

suddenly THIS
is
plenitude

lucent   bountiful

    a hundred open doorways
    door within door within:

    passage
    to unmapped terrain

In the pith of silence

pulsing beneficence

{ breath registers }

palpable